SEE IN THE DARK!

WRITTEN BY **EMILIE DUFRESNE**
DESIGNED BY **AMY LI**

BookLife
PUBLISHING

©2019
BookLife Publishing Ltd.
King's Lynn
Norfolk PE30 4LS

ISBN: 978-1-78637-616-9

Written by:
Emilie Dufresne

Edited by:
Madeline Tyler

Designed by:
Amy Li

A catalogue record for this book is available from the British Library. All facts, statistics, web addresses and URLs in this book were verified as valid and accurate at time of writing. No responsibility for any changes to external websites or references can be accepted by either the author or publisher.

PHOTO CREDITS

All images courtesy of Shutterstock. With thanks to Getty Images, Thinkstock Photo and iStockphoto.

Cover – Azamatovic, Lazerko A, UltraViolet, Zorana Matijasevic, Tiny Doz. Vector Animals – natchapohn, Andrew Rybalko (Professor Ax), Guz Anna (cat, owl), Mckenna71 (fox), natchapohn (moth), Rvector (gecko), StockSmartStart (bat, snake). Master images – TinyDoz (header font), Azamatovic, Natalisa (main and panel backgrounds), Zorana Matijasevic, UltraViolet (Comic bubbles, assets and annotations), Nata Alhontess (Speech bubbles and boxes), Lazerko A (page number cloud, stars). 1 – Lazerko A, 2-3 – Nata Alhontess, 4-5 – james weston, 6-7 – ioat, Ivan Smuk, J.D.S, Raimundo79, enjoy your life, Mio Buono, 8-9 – imaginasty, Claudia Pylinskaya, Valt Ahyppo, 10-11 – angkrit, Scott M Ward, Anna Frajtova, PinkPueblo, elenabsl, Andrew Rybalko, 12-13 – Andrew Rybalko, Roel Slootwegl, AlexandrIll, Eric Isslee, 14-15 – Dora Zett, Ivanova Krasa, mir_vam, notkoo, 16-17 – Nathapol Kongseang, ioat, YUCALORA, Anna Frajtova, 18-19 – reptiles4all, StockSmartStart, NotionPic, Ammak, 20-21 – KoDi Art, Neirfy, Sandra Standbridge, 22-23 – mhatzapa, james weston

CONTENTS

Words that look like **this** can be found in the glossary on page 24.

SUPERHEROES

OF THE FUTURE

The world is constantly under threat. Whether it's from crime, alien invasions or humans destroying the planet, one thing is known for certain. Something has got to change...

A new generation of superheroes is needed to protect the planet.

SEE IN THE DARK

Today, we will be looking for animals that can see in the dark.

These animals could use night vision, thermal vision or echolocation, and they can all see in the dark much better than most animals.

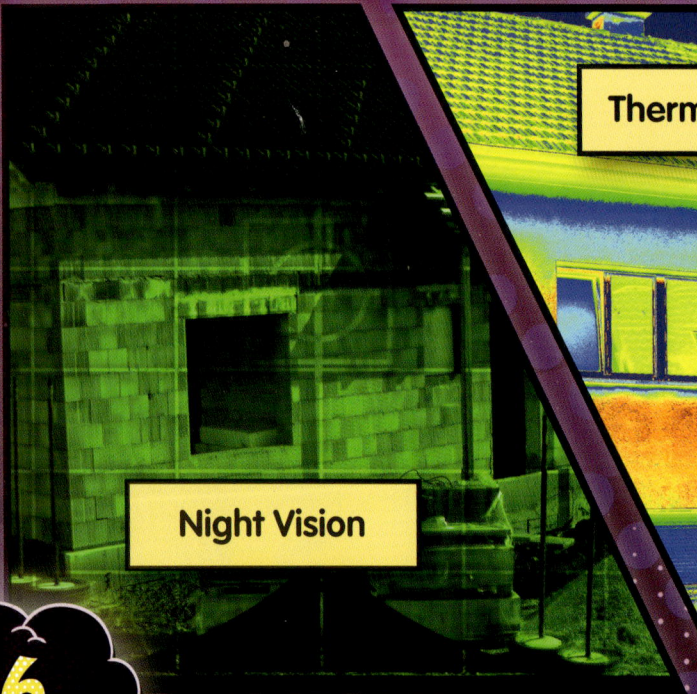

Night Vision

Thermal Vision

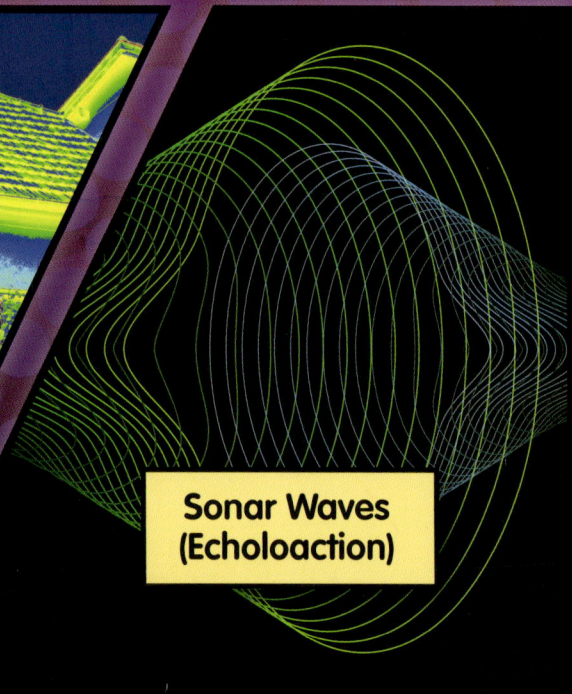

Sonar Waves (Echoloaction)

Our journey will take us all around the world. We know that there are animals with superpowers out there. Now we just need to find them.
Deserts
Cities
Forests
Professor Ax

GECKOS

First we have the leaf-tailed gecko. They are able to let more light into their eyes at night than most other animals.

In fact, they have 350 times better night vision than a human.

350x

These geckos can even see colour at night!

NAME: Leaf-tailed gecko

LIVES: Madagascar and surrounding islands

SIZE: Up to 30 centimetres (cm) long, including tail

SUPERPOWER: Clear colour vision at night

OWLS

Owls have enormous eyes that are specially adapted to see in low lighting. They can't see in colour, but they can see in very good 3D.

To protect their amazing eyes, owls have three eyelids!

Owls' eyes have lots of rod cells. These cells help owls see light and movement, even in the dark.

What letter is this?

Kyoooooo!

Rod Cell

FACT FILE

NAME:	Tawny owl	SIZE:	Up to 46 cm long
LIVES:	Europe, Asia, Siberia and Scandinavia	SUPERPOWER:	Excellent 3D vision in low lighting

FOXES

These night-dwellers have a special part in their eyes that reflects light. This makes their night vision a lot better than a human's and helps them to hunt prey at night.

Our eyes may look scary at night, but it's just reflected light!

Cats, dogs and many other mammals have these special parts in their eyes too!

12

I'm a very sensitive little fox.

It's not just their eyes that work well; their senses of smell and hearing are also excellent at night.

FACT FILE

NAME:	Red fox
LIVES:	Worldwide, across all different habitats
SIZE:	Around 80 cm nose-to-tail
SUPERPOWER:	Has reflective eyes and strong senses

In the dark, a cat's pupils grow much larger to let more light in. This makes their night-vision much clearer.

NAME: Domestic cat

LIVES: Houses all over the world

SIZE: Around 70 cm long, including tail

SUPERPOWER: Precision vision for hunting

Bats use these echoes to know where they are in the dark.

Let me use my bat detector to find one...

BAT SPOTTER 2000

kHz   kHz

FACT FILE

NAME:	Vampire bat
LIVES:	Mexico, South America and Central America
SIZE:	17 cm wingspan
SUPERPOWER:	Excellent echolocation skills

SNAKES

Snakes can see better at night than humans because they have more rod cells. However, they also have something else helping them...

Snakes can use these sensors to find a **warm-blooded** animal by following the heat it gives off.

FACT FILE

NAME:	Pit viper snake	SIZE:	Up to 3.5 metres long
LIVES:	North, Central and South America	SUPERPOWER:	Thermal night vision

They can do this by slowing down their brains. This lets them take longer to see each colour of flower and choose the right one, even in the dark.

LURRRP!

FACT FILE

NAME:	Elephant hawkmoth
LIVES:	Most common in Europe and Asia
SIZE:	6 cm wingspan
SUPERPOWER:	Able to see in colour at night

THE NEXT GENERATION

CHROMA MOTH

All of these animals are now ready to join my team, but first they need their superhero identities! Remember these faces; they might save the world one day.

PAWFECT VISION

ECHO LOCATE-EAR

RODNEY NIGHTSEER

ARE YOU A SEE-IN-THE-DARK SUPERHERO? Why not turn the lights off in your room and see how well you can see? The longer you are away from the light, the better you should be able to see in the dark!

RED THE REFLECTOR

REPT-EYES

FIRE SIGHT

23

GLOSSARY

3D	having height, width and depth
adapted	changed over time to suit the environment
cells	the basic units that make up all living things
echolocation	a process that animals, such as bats, use to locate themselves by making sounds that echo back to them
generation	a group of people that have a similar age and involved in a particular activity
mammals	animals that are warm-blooded, have a backbone and produce milk to feed their children
precision	being accurate or exact
prey	animals that are hunted by other animals for food
pupils	the dark openings in the centre of the eyes that take in light
ruthless	doing something cruel without any sympathy
thermal vision	being aware of objects in the dark by detecting heat or warmth
warm-blooded	animals that have blood that stays at a steady and warm temperature

INDEX